S0-BID-256

09/24
STRAND PRICE
$ 5.00

Classic
CONVERTIBLES

Graham Robson

CHARTWELL
BOOKS, INC.

A QUINTET BOOK

Copyright © 1995 Quintet Publishing Limited.
This book may not be reproduced in whole or in part, in any
means, electronic or mechanical, including photocopying,
recording or by any other information storage and or retrieval
system now known or hereafter invented, without written per-
mission from the publisher and copyright holder.

ISBN: 0-7858-0549-4

This book was designed and produced by
Quintet Publishing Limited

Art Director: Peter Bridgewater
Design: Jean Foley
Editor: Paul Berman, Shaun Barrington

Typeset in Great Britain by
Central Southern Typesetters, Eastbourne

Produced in Australia by Griffin Colour

Published by Chartwell Books Inc.
A Division of Book Sales, Inc.
114 Northfield Avenue
Edison, New Jersey 08837

Contents

INTRODUCTION

The attraction of open-top motoring is ideally summed up by an advert run by BL for the Triumph TR7 Convertible. A side view of the car, with soft-top furled, simply showed an arrow pointing upwards, with the punchline: 'Headroom: 93 million miles'. Quite simply, in an open-top car there is, or should be, no barrier between the driver and the rest of the world.

This book, in fact, is a celebration of a type of car which looked set to disappear ten years ago – the open-top type. Since then, of course, there has been a real revival, and a great deal of variety is once again on offer.

In the beginning, cars were sometimes known as 'horse-less-carriages', and *all* of them were open-top types of one sort or another. Quite clearly, their styles had evolved from the coachwork of horse-drawn carriages of an earlier era.

In later years, as tastes changed, and the coachbuilder's art was refined to take account of this, more and more closed cars were sold, but an increasing variety of convertible machines also became available.

Because one man's convertible is another man's drop-head coupe, one country's roadster is another country's tourer, there are two spellings of Spider/Spyder, and many other derivations on the De Ville, Landaulette, Cabriolet and Targa-roof theme, I am not about to offer a rigid definition of the convertible car. Accordingly, I have covered several different types of car in which the roof can be folded, removed, hinged – or has never actually been fitted. For that reason, therefore, a Rolls-Royce Landaulette is as much of an open-top as a Fiat X1/9, and a Cadillac Allanté is just as interesting as a Morris Minor 1000.

Ten years ago, the pundits were ready to write off the open-top car, blaming such diverse influences as United States safety legislation and the increased performance of the cars themselves, but it was never as simple as that.

Roll-over safety and the maintenance of a girl's hairstyle were both significant, of course, but not vital. The main reasons for the decline were connected with the arrival of unit-construction body/chassis units, and with the increased cost of producing limited-production specialist coachwork. Originally it was quite straightforward to produce a special body, usually based on a wood-frame skeleton, if a separate chassis provided almost all the structural stiffness. However, it was much more complicated, and costly, if there was *no* separate chassis, so that a unit-construction saloon car shell had to be re-engineered to provide open-top motoring.

Unit-construction shells were introduced for mass-production cars in the 1930s, and became dominant within 20 years. By the 1960s, open-top motoring was rapidly becoming confined to sports cars, and to the *very* expensive type of coachbuilt machine. Then, as the 1970s progressed, it began to seem that open-top cars would soon be outlawed in the USA, which meant that newly introduced sports cars like the Triumph TR7 and the Jaguar XJ-S were closed coupes, and that nothing new was coming along to replace well-loved 'classics' like the Alfa Romeo Giulia Spider and the MG MGB.

When General Motors built the last of its convertibles (Cadillac Eldorados) in 1976, pessimists were ready to write off the open-top car for good. Open-top monocoques like the MG MGB, and the Mercedes-Benz 450SL, it was suggested, were now dinosaurs, the last of the line, and the best that could be expected in the 1980s was a Porsche-style 'Targa' top, or a 'removable-roof' model like the Ferrari 308GTS.

And so it seemed – until the West Germans immediately started a new trend, with the launch of the smart new 3-Series BMW (1977) and Golf (1979) Cabriolets, both of which were based on unit-construction shells. Two years later BL launched the Triumph TR7 Convertible, a conversion of the Coupe, and the bandwagon began to roll.

The public's reaction was enthusiastic, and this was enough to encourage other makers to follow suit. Before long, other open-top cars, like the Peugeot 205 CTi, and the Porsche 911 Cabriolet, were launched, Jaguar produced an XJ-S Cabriolet, while North American makers such as Cadillac and Chrysler turned to Italy for expertise in producing large open-top models.

By the late 1980s, motoring included open-top cars as tiny as the Yugo 55 Cabriolet and as large and glossy as the Rolls-Royce Corniche, as middle-of-the road as the Ford Escort XR3i Cabriolet, and as excitingly high-performance as the Porsche 911 Turbo Cabriolet. Open-top motoring was fashionable once again, and as long as the air is still fit to breathe, its future should be assured.

GRAHAM ROBSON

RIGHT A famous Jaguar makes off, once again, for the open road. Ian Appleyard's twin-cam six-cylinder XK120 was *the* most successful rally car of the early 1950s.

ASTON MARTIN VOLANTE

PRODUCTION SPAN
1978 to date
-
ENGINE
V8, 2 ohc
-
CAPACITY
326 CID/5340cc
-
MAXIMUM POWER
309bhp (Vantage 406bhp)
-
CHASSIS/SUSPENSION
Steel platform, coil spring/
wishbone ifs, De Dion and
coil spring rear
-
BODY STYLE
2+2 DHC, by Aston Martin
-
TOP SPEED
145mph/233kph
(Vantage 170mph/273kph)
-
0–60MPH
6.2 seconds
(Vantage 5.4 seconds)
-

ABOVE The classic modern Aston Martin shape started life as a closed coupe in 1967; the convertible Volante followed in 1978.

The original Aston Martin DBS appeared in 1967, as a fastback coupe with a six-cylinder engine, but the enormously powerful 5.3-litre/326 CID V8 engine for which it had been designed made its appearance two years later. That engine, and the same basic body style, whether in closed or open-top form, were to form the basis of every Aston Martin produced in the next two decades. There was one name change, from DBS-V8, to mere 'V8', in 1972, and minor styling changes from time to time.

Even in standard-engined form it could beat 140mph/225kph, and if the fearsomely fast 'Vantage' version was ordered that top speed rose to around 170mph/273kph. In spite of its weight and bulk, it handled extremely well, though the fuel consumption was heavy. There was a choice between five-speed manual, or three-speed automatic transmissions, and the V8 was one of the few production cars in the world to use De Dion rear suspension.

Aston Martin, like other specialist car makers, always liked to have a convertible derivative of all its cars, and had first launched a 'Volante' version (which was Aston Martin's own special name for a soft-top car) of the previous range in the 1960s. It was not until 1978, however – 11 years after the coupe had first appeared – that the company offered the V8-engined Volante model.

The V8-engined car was based on a solidly engineered steel platform chassis which, because it was effectively hand-built, featured many small pressings or fabrications. Much of the body shell was steel, but many skin panels were in aluminium alloy, the whole being an intriguing blend of machine-made pressings, hand-dressed, matched, and welded together at the Aston Martin factory at Newport Pagnell. Because it was a large and wide car, the coupe was a full four-seater.

The V8 Volante, launched in June 1978, had the same basic style as the coupe, but naturally featured a power-operated soft-top, and had its floorpan stiffened to restore the rigidity of the 'chassis'. Volantes, it seemed, would take up to three months to build, and the first USA price was set at no less than $66,000. Although four full-sized seats (leather-trimmed, of course) were still provided, the folding top had encroached on the boot space, which was reduced from 8.6 cu. ft. to a mere 5.1 cu. ft.

The soft-top was, as you might expect, beautifully tailored, and when erect it turned the Volante into a snug, if somewhat claustrophobic, two-door saloon. It was just as carefully built as a Rolls-Royce. In any case a customer had a right to expect this, as he was paying similar prices.

At first the Volante was only available with the standard engine, but from 1986 an extra version, complete with deep front spoiler, was offered with the Vantage engine.

Aston Martin, which had been owned by a succession of hopeful entrepreneurs in the 1970s and 1980s, was finally taken over by the Ford Motor Co. Ltd. in 1987.

ABOVE Soft top up, or soft top down, this is a brutally impressive style. The later Volantes were also offered with the most powerful Vantage engine, and with these styling changes.

LEFT What could be better – wood, British leather, a padded steering wheel, and a speedometer reading to unimaginable levels.

AUSTIN-HEALEY 3000 MK II & MK III

PRODUCTION SPAN
1962–1967

ENGINE
6-cyl, ohv

CAPACITY
178 CID/2912cc

MAXIMUM POWER
131bhp/148bhp

CHASSIS/SUSPENSION
Ladder-style frame, steel body shell welded on assembly, coil spring/wishbone ifs, live axle and half-elliptic leaf spring rear

BODY STYLE
2+2 seater DHC, by Jensen/BMC

TOP SPEED
117mph/188kph; 121mph/195kph

0-60MPH
10.4 seconds/9.8 seconds

The Austin-Healey marque was born in 1952, and disappeared in 1970. In that time, only two different types of sports car – the small four-cylinder engined Sprite, and the larger 100/3000 range – were produced. Both were successful, and have a secure 'classic' reputation.

Donald Healey was already a famous motoring personality before he began building cars of his own design in 1946. The original 'Healeys' had Riley engines, but from 1952 the next generation was planned to use Austin engines. In a historic tie-up, his prototype Healey 100 was absorbed by the BMC combine, and the Austin-Healey marque was born.

At first the 'Big Healey' (as it eventually became known), had a four-cylinder engine, but BMC's new straight 'six' took over for 1957. This car, the 100 Six, became '3000' in 1959 with an enlarged engine, but it was not until 1962 that the body style was revised, and the true drop-head coupe was announced. All were simply built, reliable and fast.

All such Austin-Healeys were based on the same rugged chassis frame, to which the steel body shells were welded at the original assembly stage. From 1952 to 1962, however, these cars had detachable side curtains and a detachable soft-top. Some had two seats, and some were rather cramped 'occasional' 2+2 seaters. The four-cylinder cars had folding windscreens while the 'sixes' had fixed screens. All had the same graceful lines, a rather restricted ground clearance and a great deal of extrovert character. Somehow these were real he-men's cars, and have since been dubbed the last of the hairy-chested sports cars.

In 1962, the cabin was substantially re-engineered. There was a larger and curved windscreen, wind-up windows in the doors, a proper fold-away soft top with rigid rails above the door glasses and a zip-out rear window. Although all cars retained their small '+2' bucket rear seats, these had very restricted leg space, and were more useful for carrying luggage instead of people. A full-length tonneau cover was an optional extra, as was a detachable hardtop, though very few of the latter were actually sold.

Between 1962 and 1964 the rugged six-cylinder 2.9-litre/178 CID engine produced 131bhp, and the car retained the original oval-shaped instrument panel. From the beginning of 1964, until the last of the Big Healeys was built in the winter of 1967/1968, the model became Mk III.

Mk IIIs had a smart new facia style, with a wooden dashboard, a centre console between the seats and a fold-down luggage tray above the occasional rear seats. The engines were boosted to produce 148bhp, and the rear suspension was revised to give more accurate location of the axle.

During the 1960s the Austin-Healey was also developed, by the BMC factory, into a first-class competition car, supreme in high-speed rallies, and a very respectable performer in international motor racing. Many of these cars had light-alloy body panels, though all the road cars were built in pressed steel.

ABOVE The 'Big Healey' Mk III not only had wind-up windows, and a fold-down soft-top, but a wooden facia too.

RIGHT Even in the mid-1960s, the Healey 3000 retained the same basic lines as the original Austin-Healey 100 of 1952. The wind-up windows and the proper foldaway soft-top were added to the specification in 1962. This is a final-specification Mk III model.

INSERT, RIGHT From the front, the only way to differentiate a final-model 3000 Mk III from the original is by the separate side and turn indicator lamps.

BENTLEY CONTINENTAL, S-TYPE

PRODUCTION SPAN
1955–1965
∙
ENGINE
6-cyl, ohv/V8, ohv
∙
CAPACITY
298 CID/4887cc;
380 CID/6230cc
∙
MAXIMUM POWER
Not quoted
∙
CHASSIS/SUSPENSION
Ladder-style frame,
cruciform braced, coil
spring/wishbone ifs, live
axle and half elliptic leaf
spring rear
∙
BODY STYLE
5 seater DHC,
by various coachbuilders
∙
TOP SPEED
(6-cyl) 119mph/192kph;
(V8) 113mph/182kph
∙
0-60MPH
12.9 seconds/12.1 seconds
∙

The original Bentley company had been absorbed by Rolls-Royce in 1931, and the first 'Continental' model was actually a sporting version of the Rolls-Royce Phantom II of the early 1930s. It was not until the early 1950s that the 'Continental' title was applied to a Bentley.

Starting in 1945, Rolls-Royce evolved a rationalized range of chassis, in which the Bentley marque was merely a more sporting version of the Rolls-Royce of the day. Then, as later, the engines' power output was not revealed – persistent enquirers were merely answered with the suave comment that it was 'sufficient' . . . .

The post-war Bentley of 1946, the Mk IV, was the very first to have what was called a 'standard steel' saloon car body, and a Rolls-Royce equivalent, the Silver Dawn, followed a few years later.

There was still, it seemed, a healthy demand for high-performance Bentleys with a sporting character, and sleek bodywork produced by independent coachbuilders. On the R-Type chassis, therefore, the first of the Bentley Continentals was made available in 1952, and it set a trend followed in 1955 by the S-Type Continental, and during the 1970s by the Corniche.

Compared with a standard-steel Bentley, a Continental had special coachwork, still with four/five seater accommodation, and usually with two doors. Most of the cars were closed coupes, but an increasing number were ordered with convertible coachwork. Although many Bentley saloons were still chauffeur-driven, the Continental was essentially a driver's car.

Customers could direct the rolling chassis to the coachbuilder of their choice, but it was usually H. J. Mulliner, Park Ward, and James Young who got the business. Park Ward had been a Rolls-Royce subsidiary since the late 1930s, and H. J. Mulliner joined them in 1959.

Compared with the R-Type, the S-Type had a new chassis, a longer wheelbase, yet no more passenger accommodation. For the first four years the cars were powered by the long-established 4.9-litre/298 CID straight six-cylinder engine, but from late 1959 a new light-alloy V8 engine took over. Except for a very few 1955/1956 models, all had the Rolls-Royce/GM automatic transmission. Every car had drum brakes, boosted by the famous Rolls-Royce mechanical servo.

The S-Types were all large, heavy and impressive machines, with power-operated soft tops, wind-down windows in the doors, and the highest possible standards of trim, decoration and seating. Prices were very high, but so were the standards of trim. The cars were certainly more carefully built than any other of the world's luxury machines available at the time. Although an S-Type Continental was a fast car if the driver insisted (and fuel consumption, at around 15/17 Imperial mpg was very reasonable), it was more usual to see these cars used for smooth and dignified transport, around town as well as on the open road.

RIGHT The Bentley Continental S1 was built between 1956 and 1959 and was the last of the Continentals to use a six cylinder engine (in line with 8:1 compression ratio); a V8 was used for the S2 and S3 models.

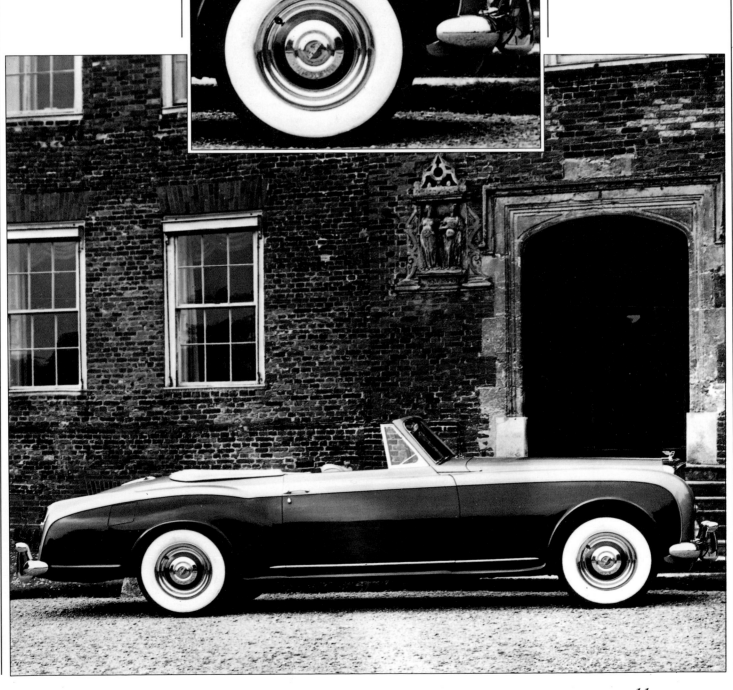

CADILLAC
CONVERTIBLES

PRODUCTION SPAN
1957–1964
-
ENGINE
V8, ohv
-
CAPACITY
365 CID/5.98 litres;
390 CID/6.38 litres;
429 CID/7.03 litres
-
MAXIMUM POWER
300/340bhp
-
CHASSIS/SUSPENSION
Separate steel chassis frame,
coil spring and wishbone ifs,
coil spring and radius arm
beam rear
-
BODY STYLE
6 seater Convertible
by Cadillac
-
TOP SPEED
(Typical) 115mph/185kph
-
0-60MPH
(Typical) 10.0 seconds approx
-

There have, of course, been many open-top Cadillacs, but none were quite so extraordinary, or so flamboyant, as those built in the 'age of the fins' period.

These cars were built at a time when the American nation as a whole, and General Motors in particular, was booming, self-confident and happy to indulge itself with extravagant consumer items. There was no functional need, and no economic reason, for giving fins to a Cadillac at this time but, what the heck, the stylists thought it made the cars look distinctive.

By the mid-1950s, Cadillac had thoroughly modernized its product line, and had an established range. All cars had V8 engines, usually with automatic transmission, and most models were in the 'Series 62' category, a group of cars which always included an open-top body option.

The Cadillac's running gear, too, had been rationalized. The cars had separate chassis frames, coil spring independent front suspension, and a live rear axle suspended on coil springs and located by radius arms. Mid-1950s engines were 365 CID/6.0-litre V8s, these being enlarged to 390 CID/6.4-litres for 1959, and to 429 CID/7.0-litres for 1964.

In the mid-1950s, Cadillac's convertible styles were all produced under the direction of Harley Earl, and it was not until the 1961 models appeared that his successor, William Mitchell, began to favour more chiselled looks, and that the image changed dramatically.

Before 1957, Cadillac rear wings had large tail-lamps with pressed steel bubbles surrounding them, but in 1957 the first of the large-finned cars appeared. In 1958 the fins were larger and the cars more bulbous (four-headlamp noses also became established), and for 1959 the height of the tail fins reached ridiculous proportions.

Then, slowly but surely, the fins began to be pared down as season followed season. The 1961 model had fins which swelled gently along the flanks from their origins on the big passenger doors. By 1963 the cars had become much more angular and slab-sided than ever, and for 1964 the fins remained only as a nostalgic reminder of the past. This was not only the last year of the fins, but also the last year of the Series 62 models.

In all these years, a Cadillac convertible was a very long car, running on a 129.5in/329cm wheelbase, and some cars weighed up to 4,700lb/2,128kg. They were all luxuriously, if somewhat garishly, equipped, all had very soft suspension which bucked and yawed on poor road surfaces, and there seemed to be power-assistance for every possible fitting. Body colours, naturally, were bright, and duo-tone treatments were often present.

A Cadillac-with-fins, in fact, represented everything that was good, and everything that was awful, about American motoring of the period. When the collectors' car boom hit the USA in the 1970s, it was inevitable that convertibles should become popular, and a well-preserved Cadillac became the most desirable of all.

OPPOSITE The birth, growth, and maturity of the Cadillac's fins – 1948 to 1961.

OPPOSITE, BELOW A 1955 Eldorado Brougham town car; note the extraordinarily aggressive bumper and the famous fins. Nothing succeeds like excess.

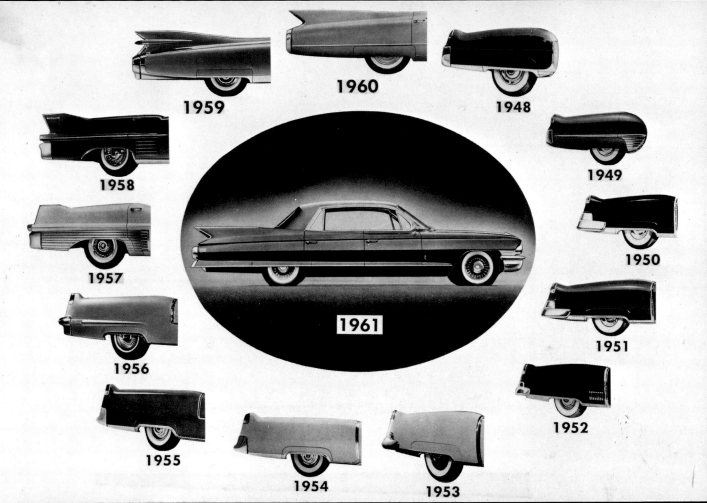

1959

1960

1948

1958

1949

1957

1950

1956

1961

1951

1955

1952

1954

1953

CHEVROLET CORVETTE

PRODUCTION SPAN
1953–1962

ENGINE
6-cyl ohv, and V8 ohv

CAPACITY
235.5 CID/3.86 litres to
327 CID/5.36 litres

MAXIMUM POWER
150 to 360bhp,
depending on engine

CHASSIS/SUSPENSION
Separate ladder-style chassis,
coil spring and wishbone ifs,
half-elliptic spring rear

BODY STYLE
2 seater Roadster, with
lift-off hardtop option,
by Chevrolet

TOP SPEED
107mph/172kph to
150mph/241kph,
depending on engine

0-60MPH
11.0 to 6.0 seconds,
depending on engine

The Chevrolet Corvette was the first two-seater sports car designed by General Motors, a company more famed for producing millions of flamboyant, but mundane, family saloons, hardtops and estate cars. The Corvette project began, in essence, as a Motorama 'one-off' show car in March 1953, but was speedily put into production.

The original Corvette production car was a rapidly, some say sketchily, developed machine, with a very basic chassis specification, a tuned-up version of Chevrolet's ubiquitous six-cylinder engine, and glass-fibre bodywork. When it became clear that the American sports car buff expected much more than this from the world's largest car-maker, development, modification and improvement began in earnest. By the early 1960s, when the next-generation Corvette (the first of the Sting Rays) was announced, the breed had been improved considerably.

From 1953 to 1962, all Corvettes were built on the same basic 102in/259cm wheelbase chassis, with rather floppy suspension. Six-cylinder engines were only used between 1953 and 1955. Chevrolet's new lightweight 'small-block' V8 engine was introduced in 1955, and was fitted to all cars from 1956 onwards. Original Corvettes were only built with automatic transmission, but a manual ('stick') option followed in 1956.

The original glass-fibre style, used until 1955, had two headlamps recessed in the front wings, a 'mouth-organ' grille, a wrap-around windscreen and detachable side-screens. For 1956 there was a completely new, larger, and more stylish body shell, with heavily sculpted sides behind the front arches, and wind-up windows; for the first time there was the option of a detachable hardtop with wrapped-round rear window. Fuel injection was offered in 1957.

The same basic body, modified to be 3in/7.6cm wider than before, and with four headlamps, was launched in 1958. This style was kept, with annual facelifts, until the end of the 1962 selling season. Every one had the severely wrapped-round windscreen and the dog-leg pillar feature which went with it. The vast majority had the fold-away soft top, but they looked smarter with the optional hardtop in place. To a whole generation of young Americans, if not to the rest of the world, this type of Corvette was the definitive open-top American car of the period.

It was not, of course, anything like the same kind of car as a European-style sports car such as a Jaguar or a Porsche. The accent was not only on form, but on embellishment and decoration, and whereas there was a good display of instruments in all these cars, there was also a great deal of glitz around them.

Even so, a well 'loaded' Corvette, with one of the very high-powered V8 engines which were optional, was a fast car by any standards, and some were equipped with fuel injection and aluminium cylinder heads. The attractiveness of the package is proven by the sales figures, which increased from 3,640 in 1954 to 14,531 in 1962.

RIGHT The original Corvette of 1953 evolved from the concept of a Motorama 'dream car', then progressively improved technically through the decade. From the beginning the body was built with glass-fibre mouldings, as on this 1954 model.

BELOW RIGHT High-style, Corvette-fashion . . . This was the instrument panel of the 1962 model.

DUESENBERG J & SJ CONVERTIBLES

PRODUCTION SPAN
1928–1937

ENGINE
8-cyl 2 ohc

CAPACITY
420 CID/6882cc

MAXIMUM POWER
200/320/400bhp

CHASSIS/SUSPENSION
Separate steel chassis frame,
half-elliptic leaf springs
front beam, half-elliptic
leaf spring and radius arm
beam rear

BODY STYLE
2 seater and 4 seater bodies,
including Convertibles by
specialist coachbuilders

TOP SPEED
Up to 135mph/217kph,
depending on engine

0-60MPH
Down to 10.0 seconds,
depending on engine

Because they were designed without an eye to cost, the Model J and SJ Duesenbergs were the most magnificently engineered US cars of the inter-war period. It was, and is, a lasting miracle that such an expensive and flamboyant motor car could continue to be sold through the depths of the Depression. Most of these cars have survived to this day.

This car, the undisputed 'King of the Classics', was engineered by Fred Duesenberg, whose company was owned by E. L. Cord. Cord's brief to him was simple – he wanted it to be the best-engineered, and the fastest, car in the world. Cord wanted to be able to sell a car which was as magnificent as a Bugatti Royale, and as well-regarded as a Rolls-Royce. Duesenberg therefore evolved a brand-new and quite peerless engine, in a conventional chassis with a choice of long – and extremely long – wheelbases (142.5in/362cm or 153.5in/390cm).

The previous Duesenberg (Model A) engine had been advanced enough, so the new unit had to be exceptional. Fred Duesenberg therefore created a 6.9-litre/420 CID, twin-overhead-cam, four-valves-per-cylinder colossus, which produced 200bhp in its most basic form, and 320bhp in SJ (S=Supercharged) form. Even the 'basic' Model J could beat 110mph/177kph, and the SJ was good for more than 120 or even 125mph/201kph.

Bodies, by the very best of American coachbuilders, were stunning, and quite unmatched by any other car maker. And so they should have been: in 1928 when the car was announced, a Model J chassis *alone* cost $8,500 (this rose to $9,500 from 1932), while average 'ready to roll' prices were around $15,000 – at least double that asked for a current V16-engined Cadillac.

A typical coachbuilt Duesenberg shell had a proud radiator which looked uncannily similar to that of a 'W.O.' Bentley, and carried twin spare wheels in pouches in the flowing wings above and behind the front wheels themselves. Wire-spoke wheels were normal wear, and the bonnets were so regally long and so high that it helped to be a tall driver.

Some cars had saloon (sedan) bodies, but many had beautifully equipped drop-head coupe bodywork. At this price, of course, Duesenberg was happy to provide any sort of body that its rich and exclusive customers demanded. Some had dickey-seats and cramped main passenger compartments, some had full-length open-top styles, and a handful had rakish roadster styles.

The American film stars Clark Gable and Gary Cooper took delivery of short-chassis SSJs, with roadster bodies. Thirty-six SJs were sold, and near the end of the production run there were a few Model JNs, but the original-type Model Js were the most numerous. All in all, 470 cars were produced in nine years, and it was the financial collapse of E. L. Cord's empire which finally killed off these fabulous creations.

OPPOSITE The early 1930s Duesenbergs – this was a 1933 Speedster – were as magnificent as any motor car so far built in the USA, and faster than any other car in the world.

INSET, OPPOSITE Every detail of the Duesenbergs was meant to indicate power, style, and wealth. Can one detect a touch of W.O. Bentley in the radiator shape?

FERRARI DAYTONA SPIDER

PRODUCTION SPAN
1969–1974
-
ENGINE
V12, 2 ohc
-
CAPACITY
268 CID/4390cc
-
MAXIMUM POWER
352bhp
-
CHASSIS/SUSPENSION
Separate multi-tubular
chassis frame, coil spring
and wishbone ifs, coil spring
and wishbone irs
-
BODY STYLE
2 seater Convertible,
by Scaglietti
-
TOP SPEED
174mph/280kph
-
0-60MPH
5.4 seconds
-

Ferrari built a series of stunning front-engined supercars in the 1960s, but none was more outstanding than the definitive example, the famous Daytona. Like most of Ferrari's two-seaters, this was conceived as a fixed-head coupe, but a Convertible (or, as the Italians usually describe it, a 'Spider') was developed later.

The Daytona's chassis was a development of that originally designed for the 275GTB model of 1964. This was the first ever Ferrari road car to have independent suspension at front *and* rear, and it was also distinguished by the use of a front-mounted V12 engine and a combined gearbox/final drive transaxle at the rear.

The first 275GTBs had single-cam V12s, the later cars twin-cam units, but the Daytona chassis which followed not only had a twin-cam V12, but a much larger one – 4.4-litres/268 CID, with no less than 352bhp. Like the late-model 275GTBs, engine and transaxle were rigidly tied together by a large-diameter torque tube.

The Daytona's body style, by Pininfarina, was simply stated and gorgeous; the car had a long and low nose, originally with headlamps hidden behind a transparent panel, a sharply raked windscreen and a smoothly tapering roof over the two seats. Luggage space was limited. The coupe itself was announced in the autumn of 1968, and like all Ferraris of the period the bodies were produced in quantity by Scaglietti in Modena.

The launch of an open-top version was inevitable, and the prototype actually appeared at the Frankfurt Motor Show of September 1969. Few modifications were needed for Pininfarina to convert the coupe to a convertible, the open-topped car retaining the same screen, the same doors and winding windows, and the same general proportions, including the straight-through crease along the flanks. Cars sold in the USA always had a different type of nose in which pop-up headlamps were used, and this feature spread to cars built for all other markets by 1971.

The Daytona not only looked magnificent, but had astonishing performance, roadholding and character. Though the Spider version might not have had quite as high a top speed as the coupe, the Daytona was one of the fastest front-engined road cars ever built, which speaks volumes for its aerodynamic efficiency.

It was an enthralling experience to drive around behind the splendid V12 engine, which was at once very powerful and very docile, beautiful to look at *and* made all the right sort of urgent tappety noises that a Ferrari buff desires. A Daytona Spider, soft top down, was the ideal sort of car for a rich man to use for cruising along sun-drenched highways.

It was, however, the last of its kind, for the front-engined Daytona was eventually displaced by the mid-engined Boxer, which was only ever sold as a closed car.

LEFT Some Ferrari styling themes were carried on, lightly modified and improved, from model to model, and there was always Pininfarina's detailing to hold it all together. The Daytona's front end featured turn indicators, parking lights, bumpers and sheet metal in a delicately sculpted whole.

BELOW For many this was the ultimate Ferrari convertible – for the 365GTS/4 was the last front-engined Ferrari V12 which also offered open-top motoring. The GTS was much more rare than the fastback GTB/4 – and today it is much more valuable. Have a look at the styling, consider the performance, and surely you can see why.

FERRARI DINO 246GTS

PRODUCTION SPAN
1972–1973
-
ENGINE
V6, 2 ohc
-
CAPACITY
148 CID/2418cc
-
MAXIMUM POWER
195bhp
-
CHASSIS/SUSPENSION
Separate multi-tubular
chassis frame, coil spring
and wishbone ifs, coil spring
and wishbone irs
-
BODY STYLE
2 seater Convertible,
by Scaglietti
-
TOP SPEED
148mph/238kph
-
0-60MPH
7.1 seconds
-

The first mid-engined Ferraris were all racing cars — single-seaters or sports prototypes — and the evolution of a road car followed on from that. The first sports-racing Dino (the name is that of Enzo Ferrari's only son, who died in 1956) appeared in the 1960s, using a completely new design of twin-cam V6 engine, and it was a later development of this engine which was also chosen for the road cars.

The first prototype coupe was shown in 1965, with the engine longitudinally mounted behind the two seats. The production car, which looked the same and was at first called the 206GT, had a light-alloy 2.0-litre/121 CID engine which was transversely mounted and drove the rear wheels through a combined gearbox/transaxle.

In 1969 the 206GT was replaced by the 246GT, which had an enlarged iron-block V6 engine, and a slightly longer wheelbase, but the style and engineering were otherwise identical. This was the chassis used until 1973, and for the last two years there was also an open-top version, the 246GTS.

Both cars used the same type of multi-tubular chassis frame, in which the passengers sat well forward. The waistline was so low that Pininfarina had to shape large wheel arch bulges over the fat tyres, the result being a sensuous little car which sold very well indeed.

Because of its mechanical layout — the engine/transmission pack was tucked in very close behind the seats — the 246GTS could not be a full convertible. Instead, Ferrari, in conjunction with Pininfarina, copied Porsche's 'Targa' idea, merely giving the car a removable roof panel, and the option of stretching a soft top — between the screen rail and the rigid bodywork behind the seats — to keep out the rain.

The Dino, whether sold as a coupe or a spider, broke new ground for Ferrari in many ways. Most important of all was that it was not *officially* a Ferrari at all, but a Dino, for the cars were not sold with Ferrari badges. This fiction, encouraged by Enzo himself to preserve the memory of his son, didn't last long with Ferrari enthusiasts, many of whom added Ferrari badges, and all of whom called the car a Ferrari anyway!

Not only that, but the Dino was the first V6-engined Ferrari road car, and the first to use a mid-engined layout. It was also the smallest-engined Ferrari for many years, as all previous road cars had been V12 monsters, some with 4.4-litre/268 CID or even 4.9-litre/303 CID displacement.

In many ways, therefore, this was the 'budget' price Ferrari (if such a thing was possible!), aimed squarely at the Porsche 911 market. With rather more attention to quality control, and with a bigger dealer network, it would have sold even better — even so it was the best-selling Ferrari so far put on sale. After the 246 range was dropped in favour of the new V8-engined cars, the famous V6 engine/transmission pack also found a home in Lancia's enormously successful Stratos competition car.

OPPOSITE The Dino's engine had an impeccable pedigree designed by Jano for racing, productionized and produced in numbers for Fiat, and used to power Ferrari and Fiat Dinos. The V6 engine had four overhead camshafts, produced plenty of torque and power, and made the most exquisite noises. From any angle, the Ferrari Dino was a gorgeous little two seater; no-one could fault the Pininfarina lines. The Spider version kept almost all of the same lines as the coupe; the only 'open-top' area was above the seats.

RIGHT The 308-328 series of Ferrari
used the same basic chassis as the
Dino of 1967-1973, but were fitted
with a newly designed 90-degree
V8. Styling, need it be said, was by
Pininfarina, another timeless
shape built in both coupe and
convertible types.

FERRARI
328GTS

PRODUCTION SPAN
1985 to date
∎

ENGINE
V8, 2 ohc
∎

CAPACITY
194 CID/3186cc
∎

MAXIMUM POWER
270bhp
∎

CHASSIS/SUSPENSION
Separate multi-tubular
chassis frame, coil spring
and wishbone ifs, coil spring
and wishbone irs
∎

BODY STYLE
2 seater Convertible,
by Scaglietti
∎

TOP SPEED
153mph/246kph
∎

0-60MPH
5.5 seconds
∎

To replace its successful V6-engined Dino series, Ferrari decided to retain the same basic mid-engined chassis layout, but to produce a new engine. Starting in 1973, therefore, the 246GT engine was replaced by the 308GT unit, a powerful new 2.9-litre/179 CID V8 engine.

Within two years Ferrari were selling Bertone-bodied 2+2 seaters, and Pininfarina-styled two-seater coupes, the latter known as the 308GTB. Two years later, in 1977, the 308GTS Spider, effectively the successor to the open-topped Dino 246GTS Spider, was also launched. Except that the Bertone car was eventually replaced by the Pininfarina-styled 2+2 Mondial in 1980, this range of V8-engined Ferraris continued in production into the late 1980s.

Ferrari had to fight hard to keep its cars abreast of USA exhaust emission laws, one result being that the V8 engine was given fuel injection in 1980, and heads with four valves per cylinder in 1982. The next important change, phased in from the autumn of 1985, was that the engine was enlarged to 3186cc/194.5 CID. The result of all these changes was that 12 years after the original 308GT engine was announced, the engine had grown, and was just 15bhp and 15lb ft of torque sharper than before.

Pininfarina's 308GTB/GTS style was acknowledged as an all-time-classic shape, right from the start. By the late 1980s it had still not been necessary to change a single major panel because the Americans, in particular, loved it just as much as they had done in the mid-1970s.

In many ways the 308GTB/GTS was merely a refinement of the previous generation 246GT/GTS type, with less pronounced wheel arch bulges, and slightly more angular lines around the tail. Ducts into the engine bay, positioned ahead of the rear wheels, were fed by air along the flanks through sculptured channels in the door pressings, while there was a low and wide nose channeling air into the front-mounted radiator. At the rear, the tail was sharply cut off, very much after the style of the legendary Daytona. The sail panels linking roof to rear quarters were arguably more elegantly treated than those of the Jaguar XJ-S.

As with the earlier Dino, the GTS Spider was really no more than a GTB with a removable roof panel; the screen and the rear quarter styling were retained for both cars. The GTS, like the GTB, had wind-up windows and even with the top removed was a draught-free car at very high cruising speeds.

The 308/328 V8 engine was as powerful, sounded just as exciting, and was as reliable as any other Ferrari unit. It was originally the first engine from Maranello to use cogged belt drive for its camshafts.

By the late 1980s, even though it was not available with four-wheel drive, anti-lock brakes or other high-tech developments, the 328GTS was still seen as one of the world's most desirable open-top machines. A successor, when it came, would have to be truly outstanding.

ABOVE The 308/328GTC models were extremely popular in the United States – in California especially – but were less common in Europe.

LEFT Ferrari's 90-degree four-cam V8, launched in 1973, was the very first V8 to be sold by the Italian company. It originally had two valves per cylinder, but by the early 1980s it had been given four-valve heads and fuel injection.

FORD
THUNDERBIRD
2-SEATER

PRODUCTION SPAN
1954–1957

ENGINE
V8, ohv

CAPACITY
256 CID/4.19 litres;
292 CID/4.78 litres;
312 CID/5.11 litres

MAXIMUM POWER
160 to 340bhp,
depending on tune

CHASSIS/SUSPENSION
Separate chassis frame, coil
spring and wishbone front,
half-elliptic spring and
beam rear

BODY STYLE
2 seater Convertible,
by Ford

TOP SPEED
(Typical: 225bhp)
113mph/182kph

0-60MPH
(Typical: 225bhp)
10.2 seconds

For some years after the Second World War, Ford-USA concentrated on building hundreds of thousands of large, reliable family cars. It was only after Ford's rival, General Motors, unexpectedly put the two-seater Chevrolet Corvette on sale, that Ford was inspired to react; the famous Thunderbird two-seater was the result.

Like the Corvette which preceded it, and the Mustang which was to follow in the 1960s, the Thunderbird was a stylish new sporting car which drew heavily on existing corporate parts already used in other models. The Thunderbird, however, had a new 102in/259cm wheelbase chassis frame, allied to a smart new body style which, in the American fashion of the day, had barrel sides, a 'straight-through' wing line from headlight to tail-lamp cluster, and a fully wrapped-round windscreen with a pronounced 'dog-leg' pillar. Detachable spats covered the rear wheels, and there were styled air vents in the tops of the front wings and on the bonnet panel. Unlike most European sports cars, the Thunderbird had a bench seat.

Although the running gear came from other Fords, with several different overhead valve V8 engine options, and with a choice of manual or automatic transmissions, the styling was at once different and refreshingly crisp. All these first-generation Thunderbirds were two-seater convertibles with capacious boot accommodation, and there was a detachable hardtop available as an option. This top, which turned the car into a wind- and waterproof two-seater saloon, was plain-panelled at first, but from 1956 there was the option of circular portholes in the rear quarters. 1955 models had spare wheels in the boot area, but for 1956 this was placed outside in front of the rear bumper, aping the Lincoln Continental Mark I which was already such a legend in American motoring history.

Ford, of course, wanted to see their new Thunderbird annihilate the Corvette, and in sales terms it certainly did; they would also have liked to kill off the imported sports cars from Europe. The new Ford, however, was too large (it weighed more than 3,000lb/1,360kg) and too softly sprung to behave like a European sports car, although it was also a fast car with a great deal of charm.

Even though the Thunderbird was outselling the Corvette by a factor of four to one, Ford management was determined to drive it upmarket and make it larger when the time came for a restyle. The second-generation Thunderbird of 1957 ran on a much longer, 113in/287cm wheelbase and was a full four-seater. Nor was the replacement car a sports car, but something which Ford called a 'personal' machine. This, together with the more obvious charms of the 1955–1957 variety, explains why a two-seater Thunderbird became a collector's piece in the 1970s, when auto nostalgia was at its height.

RIGHT Latter-day enthusiasts can always identify a late-model two seater Thunderbird by the 'porthole' option in the detachable hardtop. This became available in 1956, but just to confuse those enthusiasts, some earlier cars were treated to the porthole top by their proud owners.

BELOW RIGHT The last of the two-seater Thunderbirds was built in 1957, after which Ford produced a much larger, less sporty four seater. The '57 typified the love of glitz which marks that period, though the fins, thank goodness, never reached excessive heights.

FORD FAIRLANE 500 SKYLINER

PRODUCTION SPAN
1956–1959

ENGINE
V8, ohv

CAPACITY
272 CID/4.46 litres to
352 CID/5.77 litres

MAXIMUM POWER
190 to 300bhp

CHASSIS/SUSPENSION
Separate chassis frame, coil
spring and wishbone front,
half-elliptic spring and
beam rear

BODY STYLE
5 seater Hardtop/
Convertible, by Ford

TOP SPEED
90mph/145kph to
110mph/177kph,
depending on engine

0–60MPH
15 to 10 seconds,
depending on engine

For many years there was a Fairlane in Ford-USA's model lineup, a popular 'full-size' range of cars which in almost every case followed the accepted design convention of the day. By the mid-1950s this meant that a Fairlane was a roomy five/six-seater with lots of power, sloppy road-holding and a long list of optional extras. All cars of this type were sold as saloons, convertibles, estate cars and sometimes as pick-up trucks.

Then, in 1956, Ford astonished the motoring establishment by unveiling the Skyliner, which had a body style never before attempted (and never copied since). In short, this could look like a conventional two-door hardtop saloon – except that at the touch of a button it could turn itself into a fully open convertible. This, incidentally, was achieved while retaining the normal exterior style of a late-1950s Fairlane, and without help from advanced electronics.

The Skyliner was the only example of the retractable hardtop roof ever put on sale. When the roof was unclipped from the screen rail and the electro-hydraulic mechanism was then activated, the large boot lid opened up (it was hinged at the rear, rather than at the front), the roof neatly folded down its front few inches, after which the whole top retracted into its hiding place in the boot. The boot lid then closed, and the transformation was complete.

It was an astonishing offering which, unhappily, could embarrass its owner if any of the sequence-controlled mechanism misbehaved. There was also the inescapable problem that, with the roof retracted. there was very little stowage space of any kind, which was ludicrous for a car measuring about 210in/533cm from stem to stern. At a time when Fairlanes cost about $2,600, the extra cost of $400 for the unique retracting roof style deterred many customers, yet more than 47,000 were produced.

In all other respects, the Skyliner was just a conventional Ford of the period, which is to say that it had a separate chassis frame, with soft, long travel, suspension, the accent being on a good 'town' ride rather than firm balance at high speeds. The brakes, frankly, were poor – but so were they on other American cars of the period.

Up front there was a wuffly and dead-reliable V8 engine, usually matched to an automatic transmission. Many had 'comfort' options including electric seat adjustment, electric drop windows, a radio (not standard in those days) and much more.

Ford styling, at this time, was at its most expansive, with a wide-mouth front grille, swooping chrome 'wing' lines along the sides and rear wings which changed from sharp in 1957 to bulbous and rather more muted in the next two seasons. The windscreen had a strong 'dog-leg' feature, and there were bench seats at front and rear.

All in all, this was a fascinating car, a unique offering which could only have been born out of blasé confidence. As one historian later commented, it was 'a reminder of an age when Detroit thought it could do anything'.

RIGHT The roof was hinged so that it rose, then moved backwards, as the furling process continued.

BELOW RIGHT The Skyliner's front corner style was so typical of the period – heavily sculptured and decorated.

BELOW Amazing, but true – the Fairlane Skyliner had a retractable steel roof, which folded in an ingenious manner, and was stowed in the boot. If the electrical sequencing went wrong the owner was in serious trouble. . .

FORD MUSTANG

PRODUCTION SPAN
1964–1973
—
ENGINE
6-cyl, ohv, and V8, ohv
—
CAPACITY
170 CID/2.78 litres to
429 CID/7.02 litres
—
MAXIMUM POWER
98 to 375bhp
—
CHASSIS/SUSPENSION
Unit-construction body/
chassis structure, coil spring
and wishbone front, half-
elliptic spring and beam rear
—
BODY STYLE
5 seater Convertible,
by Ford
—
TOP SPEED
100mph/161kph to
125mph/201kph,
depending on engine
—
0-60MPH
12.5 seconds to 6 seconds,
depending on engine
—

Without much doubt, the Mustang was the single most famous Ford car introduced in the USA after the Second World War. Conceived in the early 1960s, and put on sale in 1964, it broke every sales record in the book over the next few years. It inspired Ford's main competitor, General Motors, to develop rivals, with Chrysler and American Motors eventually following suit. Ford of Europe were to draw heavily on Mustang experience when designing the Capri.

Lee Iacocca, now sometimes known as 'the father of the Mustang', saw the need for a simple, relatively small, but fast and sporty car to sell to the growing number of young drivers. Except for the limited-production Chevrolet Corvette, he reasoned, there was no domestic sporty car in the USA; the new car could fill a yawning gap.

And so it did. By American standards, not only was the Mustang cheap and cheerful, but it was sold in an astonishing number of versions. The meekest of all had six-cylinder engines, the most extrovert had vast, rumbling, gas-guzzling V8s. Some had hardtop bodies, some were fastbacks and a great number were convertibles. All of them had four-seater accommodation.

The Mustang was quick and easy to develop because it drew all its running gear from Ford's corporate 'parts bin'. The dreary Falcon, in particular, was a principal source, but the biggest and most powerful V8s came from the largest Fords then being built or planned.

Only the unit-construction body styles were unique, and had to be specially developed. The first Mustang rode on a 108in/274cm wheelbase, but this was stretched by an inch (2.5cm) for 1971. Lengths gradually crept up from 181.6in/461cm in 1964, to 189.5in/481cm for 1971. The original 1964 style was re-skinned for 1967; there was another re-style for 1970, and this model became the largest Mustang of all for the 1971–1973 period.

Each of these cars remained faithful to the long bonnet/short tail style of the original, though at each facelift the shell became smoother, the lines sleeker, and the tail higher and looking somehow more bulky. All of them were two-door models with wind-up windows. The convertibles looked much better when new, and when the soft tops fitted properly; somehow, there was nothing quite so tacky as a beaten-up Mustang convertible which had been neglected.

All the most desirable Mustangs had large-capacity V8 engines, 'four on the floor' (a four-speed manual gearbox with floor-mounted change speed lever), fat tyres and all manner of dress-up kits. Limited production types, such as the super-tuned Shelby GT350/GT500 models, and cars fitted with 'Boss' or 'Mach 1' engines, were even more popular in later life than they had been when new.

The Mustang was a car which was absolutely right for the 1960s, but not for the economy-conscious era which followed. The Mustang II which took over for 1974 was a much smaller, slower and less exciting car altogether.

LEFT By the early 1970s the original Mustang concept had been lost. The car had become bigger, leaner, but not faster. It was, nevertheless, a very attractive soft-top indeed.

BELOW The original Mustang, launched in 1964, caused a sensation. It was sold in convertible, hardtop and, eventually, in fastback guise. Today's collectors choose the convertible every time.

JAGUAR XK120

PRODUCTION SPAN
1948–1954
—
ENGINE
6-cyl, 2 ohc
—
CAPACITY
210 CID/3442cc
—
MAXIMUM POWER
160/180bhp
—
CHASSIS/SUSPENSION
Ladder-style chassis frame
with cruciform, torsion bar
ifs, elliptic leaf spring rear
—
BODY STYLE
2 seater Roadster or
Drop-head Coupe, by Jaguar
—
TOP SPEED
120mph/193kph
—
0-60MPH
10 seconds
—

William Lyons began his business career in Blackpool, with a company building special bodies for motorcycle sidecars. It was a natural progression to produce special bodies for cars, then to launch the SS car, and finally to produce the SS-Jaguar in 1935.

During the Second World War, Mr. Lyons not only planned a series of new models, but an exciting family of twin-cam engines to power them; these were called XK units, and were to be built in Coventry for the next 38 years. Although he had wanted the first new model to be a saloon car, post-war tooling bottlenecks got in the way, and the very first XK-engined car to meet its public was the XK120 sports car of 1948. It was at that time the fastest production sports car in the world.

In the drab, post-war, car-starved world of 1948, the beautifully styled XK120 caused a real sensation, and although Jaguar had intended to produce it only in limited numbers, those plans were soon expanded, and from 1950 the 160bhp two-seater was available in larger quantities. Many of the cars were sold in the USA, thus founding the Jaguar cult which has persisted to this day.

The XK120 was new from end to end, with torsion bar independent front suspension on a 102in/259cm wheelbase, the extremely powerful and very impressive-looking engine, and of course its remarkable looks. Not only did these cars look wonderful, but they were extremely fast *and* they seemed to make all the right noises.

All previous Jaguars had used 1930s-type looks, with long flowing wings, running boards under the doors and free-standing headlamps, but the new XK120 was much more 'continental' in its looks, with full-width styling, curvaceous but graceful flanks and a narrow front grille with the headlamps tucked away at each side.

The original XK120 was sold only as a two-seater Roadster, and had aluminium bodywork built up on a wooden framework, but from 1950 a new and fully tooled pressed-steel shell took its place; the actual styling was not changed. This car had a simple foldaway soft top which sat rather high over the vee-screen, and there were removable side curtains on the cutaway doors. A neat fixed-head coupe version followed in 1950, but it was not until April 1953 that the extremely well-equipped drop-head coupe appeared. This car had a tailored and padded soft top with a fully fitted interior, and there were different doors, with opening quarter windows and wind-up glass.

The XK120, of course, was only the first of three different XK production models, for in 1954 the XK120 was replaced by the more powerful, better-handling and even better-equipped XK140, which looked almost the same as before, while in 1957 the XK150 was a rather more matronly derivative of the style, with a curved single-piece screen, but still on the original chassis. The last of the XK sports cars was built in the winter of 1960/1961, and its even more memorable successor was the E-Type.

OPPOSITE, LEFT By the early 1950s, the original XK120 Roadster had been joined by the very smart, and well-trimmed, Drop-Head Coupe.

OPPOSITE, CENTRE The coupe still lacked the rear bumper protection which American buyers needed.

OPPOSITE, RIGHT In spite of its flashing performance, and graceful exterior style, the XK120 Drop-Head Coupe retained a traditional British type of wooden facia, with a four-spoke steering wheel, and wind-up door windows.

OPPOSITE, BELOW The front-end detail of all XK120s was exquisite, with not a straight line in sight. Later XKs took their inspiration from this layout too.

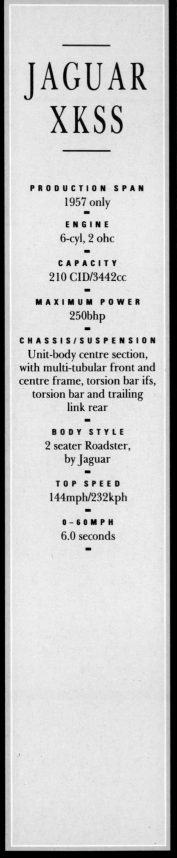

JAGUAR XKSS

PRODUCTION SPAN
1957 only
-
ENGINE
6-cyl, 2 ohc
-
CAPACITY
210 CID/3442cc
-
MAXIMUM POWER
250bhp
-
CHASSIS/SUSPENSION
Unit-body centre section,
with multi-tubular front and
centre frame, torsion bar ifs,
torsion bar and trailing
link rear
-
BODY STYLE
2 seater Roadster,
by Jaguar
-
TOP SPEED
144mph/232kph
-
0-60MPH
6.0 seconds
-

Jaguar's famous and very rare XKSS – only 16 cars were built – became legendary although it was a marketing failure. It was, in any case, a car developed to 'use up' a stock of D-Type racing sports cars, and even then it took a long time to sell the small number produced. Perhaps it was a blessing that a factory fire put a stop to the possibility of building any more.

Jaguar, having launched the famous twin-cam XK engine in 1948, soon got involved in sports-car racing, first with modified XK120s, and from 1951 with the specially developed XK120C, or C-Type, competition car. Then, in 1954, Jaguar produced the racing D-Type, initially as a 'works' racing car, and from 1955 as a limited-production machine for worldwide sale.

Unhappily for Jaguar, more D-Types were built than could be sold, so at the end of 1956 a bold decision was taken – the unsold stock of D-Types would be lightly re-worked, and sold as 'road-going' cars called XKSS. There was no question of these race-proved and very starkly equipped machines being de-tuned – they were merely given better weather protection, a bit more passenger space and a new image.

The D-Type had been built around a wind-cheating oval-shaped cross section, with the two seats demanded by international regulations, but very limited leg room for the 'passenger' who, if carried, had no screen ahead of him, for there was only a piece of perspex wrapped around the driver's side, and a headrest behind his head.

For the XKSS conversion, which was not really intended as a road car, but as a machine for use in USA 'production-car' racing, the D-Type was given a full-width curved wind-screen, the headrest and the metal spine between the body seat cut-outs were removed, a second door was added to the left side and fixed sidescreens were added to those very steeply contoured but tiny doors. Smart (though function-ally insignificant) bumpers were added at front and rear, a luggage rack was fixed to the top of the tail and a fold-down soft top was also added. Because the entire front end was hinged at the nose, there was excellent access to the engine bay and front suspension for maintenance work.

All this turned the D-Type into a rather more habitable machine, but there were still many 'race only' features – no heating, no stowage space inside the car, and a fuel filler hidden *inside* the soft top, which therefore had to be folded down before the car could be re-fuelled in wet weather! The so-called silencer was still no more than a gesture to regulations, and the overall effect was of an ultra-rapid Supercar which could be used on the public highway if its rich owner was so inclined.

The XKSS, like the D-Type, looked beautiful because of its elegant and well-curved styling. Most of the running gear was adapted from that used in Jaguar road cars, and this explains why so many 'replica' cars of this most charis-matic machine have been constructed in recent years.

CENTRE, TOP When Jaguar converted D-Types into XKSS 'road cars', it discarded the hump behind the driver's head, added a full-width screen, and a fold-down soft top.

CENTRE, MIDDLE The XKSS, like the D-Type from which it was derived, had a magnificent 250bhp version of the six-cylinder XK engine, complete with three Weber twin-choke carburettors.

CENTRE, BELOW 'The office' of the XKSS was slightly more civilised than that of the D-Type, but still had restricted leg room, and virtually nowhere to stow anything. But with all that performance in reserve, no-one seemed to care. . . .

BELOW Jaguar's rare, and exclusive, XKSS, was no more than a road-equipped version of the D-Type racing sports car. For road use, however, the car was given a full-width wrap-around screen, side-curtains for the doors, and a rather flimsy-looking bumper.

JAGUAR E-TYPE

PRODUCTION SPAN
1961–1975
-
ENGINE
6-cyl, 2 ohc, and V12, ohc
-
CAPACITY
230 CID/3781cc;
258 CID/4235cc;
326 CID/5343cc
-
MAXIMUM POWER
265bhp/272bhp
-
CHASSIS/SUSPENSION
Unit-body centre section,
with multi-tubular front
frame, torsion bar ifs,
coil spring wishbone and
fixed-length drive shaft irs
-
BODY STYLE
2 seater Roadster or Coupe,
or 2+2 Coupe, by Jaguar
-
TOP SPEED
150mph/241kph
(146mph/235kph for V12)
-
0-60MPH
7.0 seconds
(6.5 seconds for V12)
-

Jaguar built the XK family of sports cars for more than 12 years. In that time, technology had advanced apace, and so had Jaguar's thinking. In place of the conventional XK models, Jaguar introduced the sexily styled E-Type, which made headlines all round the world.

A new car, always coded E-Type, was actually conceived in 1956, to succeed the D-Type as a racing sports car, but following Jaguar's withdrawal from motor racing, the new model became 'softer', better-equipped, and altogether more civilized. Originally meant to be only an open two-seater, it was also developed as a fastback/hatchback coupe. Even if some of the management team doubted that it would sell in large enough quantities, it was prepared for production and put on sale in 1961.

Original E-Types had 3.8-litre/231 CID six-cylinder engines, but for 1965 the unit was enlarged to 4.2-litres/258 CID. Then, in 1971, the E-Type became the first Jaguar to use the brand-new 5.3-litre/326 CID V12 engine, a unit which had still not reached the peak of its development in the late 1980s. Every time a more powerful engine was made available, legislative changes (particularly in the USA) obliged Jaguar to de-tune once again. The result is that the V12 was really very little faster than an original 3.8-litre, though it was better developed, and more versatile.

Structurally, and in its styling, the E-Type was a further evolution of the D-Type/XKSS layout, with a monocoque centre section, a multi-tubular front end and the same sleek and flowing lines which were never successfully copied by any other car maker. Like the mid-1950s D-Type before it, the first E-Types had headlamps tucked away behind transparent covers, as well as high and rounded tails and rather minimal two-seater accommodation.

Demand for soft-top roadsters and fixed-head types was almost equally matched. The fixed-head model was arguably better styled, and had more, and certainly more useful, luggage accommodation. The Roadster, on the other hand, still had wind-up windows in its doors and a full-size curved screen, plus a folding soft top which clung to its job even at the very high speeds of which an E-Type was capable. From 1966, too, there was a longer-wheelbase version of the fixed-head car, which had extra occasional seats, and was predictably called the '2+2' model.

A well-maintained E-Type not only looked marvellous, and had the same sort of appearance as a limited-production Italian Supercar, but it also had excellent handling and brakes *and* its engine was so docile that it could be trickled gently around town, or up and down the boulevards of Los Angeles, without losing its composure.

Above all, however, it was the E-Type's styling, the feline grace of its lines and the animal-like purr, or throb, of its excellent engine which made it such an exciting proposition. When it was eventually dropped in 1975, the world of motoring grieved – and the car which took over, the XJ-S, was not at all the same type of machine.

OPPOSITE, INSET In the 1960s, the Jaguar E-Type became one of the most easily-recognized cars in the world.

RIGHT After ten years, Jaguar redesigned the E-Type, turning it into Series III with a brand new V12 engine. From this point, all types were built on the longer wheelbase underframe.

RIGHT, BELOW All E-Types had curvaceous rears, with the exhaust system taking a prominent part in the style.

FAR RIGHT, BELOW E-Type facias were comprehensively equipped. Naturally the big speedometer and rev-counter dials were placed ahead of the driver's eyes.

LINCOLN
CONTINENTAL
MK 1

PRODUCTION SPAN
1940–1948
-
ENGINE
V12, sv
-
CAPACITY
290 CID/4784cc
-
MAXIMUM POWER
120bhp
-
CHASSIS/SUSPENSION
Ladder-style chassis frame,
transverse leaf spring front
beam, transverse leaf spring
rear
-
BODY STYLE
5 seater Convertible (or
Saloon), by Ford-USA
-
TOP SPEED
85mph/137kph approx
-
0-60MPH
Not known
-

Lincoln, once a proudly independent concern, had been bought up by Ford in the 1920s, though it continued to use unique running gear for some years to come. By the late 1930s the marque had been devalued, so that a 'Lincoln' was really only an up-market Ford. Henry Ford's son Edsel, who was already president of the Ford Motor Co., decided to make Lincoln a distinctive car once again, and the original Continental of 1940 was the result.

This was the first Lincoln, for many years, in which styling and equipment took precedence over cost control. Lincoln devotees like to ignore the fact that under its elegant skin the Continental was no more than a mildly reworked Lincoln Zephyr, with the same 125in/317cm wheelbase chassis, and 75 degree side-valve V12 engine.

Suspension, as on other Fords, Mercurys and Lincolns of the period, featured transverse leaf springs and beam axles at front and rear. This was due to Henry Ford's personal edict; Edsel would have liked to emulate the competition from General Motors, which had independent front suspension. For the special Continental application, the engine was given aluminium cylinder heads, while the three-speed gearbox was joined by a two-speed Columbia rear axle. In 1942 there was a short-lived 5-litre/306 CID engine, and an unpopular 'Liquimatic' automatic transmission; a more successful overdrive option replaced the two-speed axle.

The original Continental Mk 1 (later to become known, simply, as the 'Mark') was announced in 1940, and was available either as a two-door fixed-head coupe, or a two-door convertible. At first, one of the most obvious recognition points was the use of an exposed spare wheel, but in later months this was given a cover.

At the front, the original 'Mark' looked much like every other Lincoln-Zephyr, with its headlamps recessed in the wings and with a two-part grille divided by a sharp prow over the radiator. For 1942 (which was a very short selling season, prior to entry into the Second World War), the front end was restyled, with squarer front wings.

It was in its profile – long, smooth and carefully detailed – and in its detail finish that the Mark was such an advance over any other Ford or Lincoln-Mercury product. There were no running boards, the Cabriolet soft top was superbly tailored and there was little evidence of Detroit 'jazz' in the detailing. Edsel Ford, who died in 1943, always intended that the Mark should be equal to, if not better than, the Cadillac, and in terms of style and equipment this aim certainly succeeded. This explains the fitments of the Lincoln-Zephyr Town Limousine's instrument panel, and gold-accented finish of interior trim and hardware. The cylinder heads were of polished aluminium, as were the manifolds, and even the cylinder head nuts were chrome-plated. Vacuum window lifts were fitted.

Even though the Mark sold better after the war than before it, it was dropped in 1948 when the high cost of hand-crafting the interior could no longer be justified.

RIGHT Like other Lincolns of the period, the Continental Mark 1 had a distinctive nose, featuring grilles at each side of the commanding prow.

BELOW The original Lincoln Continental, launched in 1940, was masterminded by Henry Ford's son Edsel. Although it shared its chassis and running gear with the current Lincoln Zephyr, it had a unique body style, so elegant for the period that it became an instant 'classic'.

MG TC

PRODUCTION SPAN
1945–1949
-
ENGINE
4-cyl, ohv
-
CAPACITY
76 CID/1250cc
-
MAXIMUM POWER
54bhp
-
CHASSIS/SUSPENSION
Ladder-style chassis frame,
half-elliptic leaf spring front
beam, half-elliptic leaf
spring rear
-
BODY STYLE
2 seater Roadster,
by MG
-
TOP SPEED
75mph/121kph
-
0-60MPH
22.7 seconds
-

MG's reputation for building simple and effective sports cars was built, in Oxford, in the 1920s, but it was with the launch of the first Midget, in 1928, that the appeal became universal. For the next 27 years there was always a Midget in the range, and this was always MG's best-selling model.

The T-Series dynasty was founded in 1936, following a corporate revolution at Nuffield. The TA was the first sports car designed at Morris Motors, rather than by MG itself. Except that a simpler overhead valve engine was used, the basic design layout of the car was unchanged – the TA, like the P-Series cars it replaced, had a simple chassis frame, front and rear suspension by beam axles and half-elliptic springs, and traditional body styling with sweeping front wings and free-standing headlamps.

The TA gave way to the TB in 1939, when a more modern engine was specified, but the outbreak of war soon put a stop to all MG sports-car sales. In 1945, when car assembly was resumed, the TB was lightly revised and put on sale again as the TC.

Although by that time it was beginning to look a touch old-fashioned, the TC was a great success, and introduced the MG marque to the important United States market. The TC was always a right-hand-drive car, but as it was so slim and manoeuvrable the Americans loved it anyway!

The TC was a rugged and simple little car, easy to build and equally easy to maintain. The body shell was built up around a wooden skeleton, with steel panels, and in most cases the car was used fully open. In this state, it was possible to fold the screen flat; some customers installed aero screens to give themselves a modicum of shelter.

When the weather was so bad that even a sports-car enthusiast had to hide himself away, there was a simple fold-away soft top which clipped to the screen rail and skimpy plastic side curtains which plugged into the cut-away doors and to the rear quarters behind the doors. Thus fitted out, the TC was waterproof, but by no means wind-proof, and since a heater was not usually fitted it meant that cold-climate owners had to be prepared to dress up for long journeys. Luggage, if any, was normally stowed behind the bench seat, but it was also possible to buy a luggage rack to drape over the exposed spare wheel.

The joys of MG Midget motoring were not in the straight-line performance of the car, but in the sheer joyful way that the car could be urged along twisty roads. It did not seem to matter that the suspension was very hard, nor that the tyres were narrow, for the car could almost be willed, rather than driven, round every corner.

It would not be an exaggeration to suggest that the MG TC was the car which paved the way for every other British sports car to sell so well in world markets, and it is still the model thought to be so typical of the MG marque. Yet only 10,000 TCs were built – perhaps every one of them was remembered with affection?

RIGHT The MG TC of 1945-1950 was the final flowering of a body style introduced in the early 1930s. Recognition points included the proud vertical radiator grille, the free-standing headlamps, the flowing wing line, and the exposed fuel tank and spare wheel.

BELOW RIGHT The MG TC was nothing if not practical. Side curtains could be plugged in to the doors to protect the driver in wet weather, but many owners never troubled to do this. The soft-top was a simple fold-away device which lived behind the seats when furled.

MORGAN PLUS 8

PRODUCTION SPAN
1968 to date
-
ENGINE
V8, ohv
-
CAPACITY
215 CID/3528cc
-
MAXIMUM POWER
151/153/155/190bhp
-
CHASSIS/SUSPENSION
Ladder-style chassis frame,
coil spring and sliding
pillar ifs, half-elliptic
leaf spring rear
-
BODY STYLE
2 seater Roadster,
by Morgan
-
TOP SPEED
125mph/201kph
-
0-60MPH
6.5/5.6 seconds,
depending on engine tune
-

Morgan introduced its first four-wheeler in 1935, and its styling has remained in a time-warp ever since. The type of construction has not been altered, and except for certain smoothing-out operations at the front and the rear the shape of the car is very much as before. It is often said that a new Morgan is as close to a 50-year-old 'classic' as can be found anywhere in the world.

Earlier Morgans had four-cylinder engines, latterly Triumph TR units bought from Standard-Triumph, but when the supply ran out a new engine was necessary. It was at this point that the company turned to Rover, arranged to take supplies of the light-alloy 3.5-litre/215 CID V8 unit, and the Morgan Plus 8 was born. By the late 1980s it had been on sale for nearly 20 years, without any sign of a redesign, and without any sign of flagging demand.

The Plus 8, like every other Morgan, took shape at Malvern Link around the basis of a simple, ladder-style chassis frame. This used the sliding pillar type of independent front suspension with which every Morgan had been fitted since the first tricycle had taken to the road in 1910.

Like every other Morgan, too, the Plus 8 had a very hard ride, but it was undeniably a hairy-chested sports car. Because of the huge torque available, it had astonishing acceleration, and the rush to the horizon was only eventually slowed by the old-fashioned aerodynamics.

The body shell had a wooden skeleton, to which the steel or aluminium skin panels were fixed. The stance was so low that, helped by the cutaway doors, it was possible for the passenger to put his arm out of the side of the body shell and touch the ground without straining his posture.

There was a fixed windscreen, and a simple fold-away soft top which was stowed in a pouch behind the passenger compartment. Like every other traditional Morgan, the Plus 8 had removable sidescreens, with sliding perspex panels, and a fold-out flap through which the driver could make hand signals. The seats were well-padded, but placed low, and the passengers' legs were near-horizontal, at each side of a prominent transmission tunnel.

Except for a small area behind the seats, there was no enclosed stowage compartment; most Plus 8 owners strapped their cases to a luggage rack on the tail.

Development, and change, came slowly at Morgan; but in the first 20 years the engine was gradually made more powerful, the entire gearbox was changed on two occasions, a rack-and-pinion steering installation became available and the whole car became wider to match the latest tyres and wheels.

Morgans either attract hate or adulation, but the company never found any problems in maintaining a healthy waiting list for these extrovert machines. A typical Plus 8 customer waited in line for years, got used to the bone-shattering ride and usually fell in love with the performance and the exuberant character. Then, as likely as not, he went out and ordered another one!

RIGHT Born in the 1930s, refined over the last half-century, the Morgan sports style changed only gradually from year to year. This rakish Plus 8 was actually built in 1982-1983.

FAR RIGHT The Morgan Plus Eight facia and instrument layout was logical, complete, and easy to read. Note the traditional type of cutaway doors, with pockets for map stowage.

LOWER RIGHT Except that wheels have become fatter, the front end style of the Plus Eight, complete with podded headlamps and a traditional type of chrome bumper, is just the same as it was in the mid-1950s.

PORSCHE
356
CABRIOLET

PRODUCTION SPAN
1949–1965

ENGINE
Flat-4, ohv

CAPACITY
66 CID/1086cc to
97 CID/1582cc

MAXIMUM POWER
40 to 90bhp

CHASSIS/SUSPENSION
Pressed platform chassis
structure, with steel body
shell, torsion bar and
trailing link ifs, torsion bar
and swing axle irs

BODY STYLE
2+2 seater Cabriolet,
by Beutler/Porsche

TOP SPEED
85mph/137kph to
111mph/197kph,
depending on engine

0-60MPH
15 seconds to 11.5 seconds,
depending on engine

The name of Porsche had been famous for many years before the first Porsche car was launched. Dr Ferdinand Porsche had designed many fine cars for companies including Austro-Daimler and Mercedes-Benz before setting up his own design bureau in 1930. His crowning achievement in the 1930s, however, was to design the legendary VW 'Beetle', and it was on the basis of this car that his son Ferry developed the first Porsche-badged sports car, always known as the 356 model.

The first hand-built Porsches were produced in Austria, but proper series production began in 1949 when the company re-established itself in Stuttgart, West Germany. Almost from the start, the new rear-engined Porsches were available as Coupes or as Cabriolets.

In the beginning, these cars were little more than special-bodied VW Beetles, but as development progressed the engineering became more and more special. The flat-four air-cooled engines, in particular, soon became almost pure Porsche, and were much more powerful than any engine used in a VW-badged car.

The platform chassis had its engine in the tail, driving forward to a gearbox/transaxle, while there was independent suspension at front and rear. Most of the car's weight was in the rear, which led to early Porsches having a reputation for somewhat precarious handling, with lots of tail-out oversteer.

Following up the themes of the wind-cheating Beetle and the still-born sports coupe types which had been developed for VW in the late 1930s, Porsche produced a very smooth and slippery body style. The nose was very low, the headlamps were completely faired into the front wings and there was a continuous sweep of sheet metal from nose to tail.

Most early cars were fixed head/fastback coupes, but the Cabriolet, whose top tucked neatly away when furled, but which had a very small rear window, was also popular. Because this car had a relatively high waistline and low seating, one definitely sat 'in' rather than 'on' a Porsche 356.

There were four distinctly different types of 356 – the original vee-screen cars built up until 1955, the Type 356A of 1955-1959 (which had a one-piece screen), the 356Bs of 1959-1963, with raised headlamps and bumpers and the final Type 356C of 1963-1965, which had disc brakes. In that time the engines were gradually but persistently enlarged, with many different sizes being offered along the way. The majority of surviving 356s, however, now seem to have the 1582cc/96.6 CID engine, either in 75bhp or 90bhp guise.

All these Porsches had remarkably efficient body styles (the coupe being rather more wind-cheating than the Cabriolet) and because they were also high-geared it was possible to cruise along very quickly for hours on end. A Porsche of this type, too, was not only a fast car, but a very reliable car, and most customers, having bought their first, stayed loyal to Stuttgart for many car changes to come.

OPPOSITE Over the years the Porsche 356 was produced with several different body types. The Cabriolet was on sale from the start, and was later joined by a hardtop version using the same body pressings. The engine was in the tail, and much of the chassis engineering derived from that of the VW Beetle.

RIGHT, INSET Every detail of the Porsche's styling was carefully worked out, for there was a Porsche badge on the chrome handle, which was also used to lift up the lid of the front compartment.

OVERLEAF A historic Porsche – actually the first car produced by the fledgling firm in 1948. This was a very starkly detailed machine, which was almost entirely VW Beetle under the smooth skin.

PORSCHE
911 TARGA & CABRIOLET

PRODUCTION SPAN
1965 to date

ENGINE
Flat-6, ohc

CAPACITY
121 CID/1991cc to
201 CID/3299cc

MAXIMUM POWER
130 to 300bhp

CHASSIS/SUSPENSION
Unit-construction steel body/
chassis structure, torsion
bar and MacPherson strut
ifs, torsion bar and semi-
trailing arm irs

BODY STYLE
2+2 seater open-top
'Targa', or Cabriolet,
by Porsche

TOP SPEED
137mph/220kph to
162mph/261kph,
depending on engine

0-60MPH
8.0 seconds to 5.0 seconds,
depending on engine

The Porsche 911 is probably the most successful Supercar of all time, not only for the performance which all derivatives offered, but for the reliability and service expertise built up around this long-running family of cars.

The 911 was conceived to supplement, then take over from, the long-running 356 family. It was announced in 1963 in 2.0-litre/121 CID form, and went on sale in 1964. Its design philosophy was exactly the same – rear-mounted air-cooled engine, wind-cheating style, 2+2 seating – but every single component was newly developed.

The original 911s were all 2+2-seater fastback coupes, but from the autumn of 1965 a new type of style, called 'Targa' was introduced. This, while keeping the same body lines, included a removable soft-top panel, while there was a substantial and permanently fixed roll-hoop above the occupants' heads. Even so, this was not a complete, conventional Cabriolet, and it was not until 1982 that such a fully convertible 911 was put on sale.

In its styling, the first 911 was a natural descendant of the final 356, with a low snout with headlamps at the corners, a fastback body style and a multitude of air vents in the tail. The whole car was rather wider, squatter, larger and subtly more upmarket than the earlier 356.

Over the years the style changed considerably, in detail if not in concept, for the wheelbase was slightly lengthened (which caused changes around the rear wheel arches), wheels and tyres were progressively widened (which resulted in the appearance of wheel-arch flares, front and rear), while aerodynamic 'tuning' resulted in the addition of substantial front under-bumper spoilers and a selection of large spoilers across the tail. In the same period the engine was gradually enlarged, eventually to 3.3-litres/201 CID, with a turbocharged version being sold from 1975.

The structure itself was a sturdy steel monocoque which, from the late 1970s, was largely made from galvanized panels. The engine was tucked away in the rear, and there was all-independent suspension, allied to four-wheel disc brakes and rack-and-pinion steering, to give the best possible roadholding from a layout with unpromising weight distribution. Early cars had spooky handling, but later cars, with wider wheels and tyres, were improved; the turbocharged cars were the fastest, and the best, of all.

Even though it was developed with Teutonic thoroughness, the 911 always retained a great deal of rather self-willed character. The combination of styling, performance, efficiency and above all the flat-sounding bark of the six-cylinder engine was unmatched by any rival. Time and again the 911 was rumoured to be on the verge of extinction (and indeed the front-engined 928 was originally designed to replace it), but it continued to sell as well as ever.

If Porsche was starting again, it would probably make the 911 a more spacious car with a quieter engine, but that might have resulted in a soulless car without hundreds of thousands of fanatical owners.

RIGHT Porsche put the 911 Coupe on sale in 1964, but the first open-top 'Targa' variety followed in 1965. The basic shape was not then changed for the next two decades as this study of a 1988 model confirms. The roll bar behind the seats is fixed, for only the roof panel can be removed.

FAR RIGHT A fully convertible of the famous Porsche 911 design was put on sale in 1982.

BELOW RIGHT More than 20 years after it was put on sale, the Porsche 911 still looked elegant and gracious. The engine was in the extreme tail, and even on full convertible types there was a comprehensively trimmed and equipped interior.

TRIUMPH
TR4, TR4A, TR5, TR250

PRODUCTION SPAN
1961–1968

ENGINE
4-cyl, ohv, or 6-cyl, ohv

CAPACITY
121 CID/1991cc;
130 CID/2138cc;
152 CID/2498cc

MAXIMUM POWER
83, 130 or 145bhp

CHASSIS/SUSPENSION
Separate frame, coil spring
and wishbone ifs, half-
elliptic rear on TR4, coil
spring and semi-trailing
irs on others

BODY STYLE
2 seater Roadster, or
removable-roof model,
by Standard-Triumph

TOP SPEED
102mph/164kph;
109mph/175kph;
120mph/193kph,
depending on engine

0-60MPH
10.9 seconds to 8.8 seconds,
depending on model

The first Triumph TR to go on sale was the TR2 of 1953, and the same 'side-curtain' body style then remained in production for nine years. It was with this light, rugged and characterful little car that Triumph made its reputation in the USA.

Whereas the TR2/TR3/TR3A range had been strictly conventional, even traditional, in its body layout, the car which succeeded it in 1961 was much more adventurous. Not only was the TR4 a better-equipped and more civilized machine than any previous TR, but it had particularly versatile features. The secret of the new car, which had been conceived and styled by Giovanni Michelotti in Italy, was not only that it had wind-up windows in the doors, along with face-level ventilation on the instrument panel, but also that it was the first car to use the removable-roof type of hardtop which was later credited to Porsche.

The same basic body shell was used in four TR models in the 1960s, but there were important mechanical differences between them all. The TR4 used a slightly modified version of the TR3A's 88in/223.5cm wheelbase chassis, still using the famous 'wet-liner' four-cylinder engine which was also used in the Standard Vanguard family car, and the Ferguson tractor! This chassis still had limited wheel movement and a very hard ride. In 1965, the TR4A had a new chassis, with independent rear suspension (except in the USA where an old-style beam axle was optional). Then in 1967, the TR5 and TR250 models were given smooth new 2498cc/152.5 CID six-cylinder engines (developed from the Triumph 2000), with fuel injection for the TR5 and a de-toxed engine for the TR250.

The most exciting and extroverted of all these types was the TR5, which had a genuine top speed of around 120mph/193kph, acceleration to match, and character which really required a strong-armed and strong-willed driver to get the best out of it.

In its normal 'Roadster' form, the TR4 and its successors had a normal fold-down soft top, which was covered in a bag when furled. The cars were also sold with optional hardtops, and it was here that innovation appeared. The removable hardtop was a two-piece, bolt-together item, comprising a rear section surrounding the rear window, and a complete steel roof panel which could be removed and left at home, if desired. Not only that, but a 'Surrey top' could also be supplied, which was a soft top on a light tubular frame which could be fitted in place of the steel roof panel. In full hard-top form, with steel roof in place and with windows wound up, these cars were as wind- and waterproof as a saloon, but with everything off they were still proper sports cars.

For 1969 this body shell was considerably facelifted by Karmann of West Germany to become the TR6, but there was a new and angular hardtop option, without removable panels and without the ability to chop and change according to the driver's wishes.

RIGHT The Michelotti-styled TR4 was introduced in 1961, and also provided the body style for later versions, the TR4A and the TR5/TR250 models. This is a TR5, dating from 1967, and has the optional hardtop fitted, but with the centre panel removed.

FAR RIGHT Triumph provided the original 'Targa' type of open-top motoring before Porsche re-invented it for its 911 models. The rear half of the optional hardtop is fixed to the body shell, and the roof can be a steel panel, or a canvas 'Surrey' top.

BELOW RIGHT Under the skin of all such TRs was a separate steel chassis frame. For the TR4A, the independent rear suspension was new, while the TR5 and TR250 models were the first to use six-cylinder engines.